THE GODS OF THE HILLS

Poems

P. S. HAUSER

ISBN-13: 9781546410829
ISBN-10: 1546410821
Library of Congress Control Number: 2017907862
CreateSpace Independent Publishing Platform
North Charleston, South Carolina

THE GODS OF THE HILLS

CONTENTS

PREFACE

The gods of the valley are not
the gods of the hills, ...

Ethan Allen

And the servants of the king of Syria said unto him,
Their gods are gods of the hills; therefore they are
stronger than we; but let us fight against them in the
plain, and surely we shall be stronger than they.

I Kings 20: 23 (KJV)

I will lift up mine eyes unto the hills, from whence
cometh
my help.

Psalms 121:1 (KJV)

And when he had sent the multitudes away, he went up
into a mountain apart to pray: and when the evening was
come, he was there alone.

Matthew 14:23 (KJV)

And he carried me away in the spirit to a great and
high mountain, and shewed me that great city, the
holy Jerusalem, descending out of heaven from God,

Revelation 21:10 (KJV)

Allen's defiance rings clearly and resonates deeply. It is a call to
independence. It is the cry of all Highlanders against the corrupting,
red-eyed deities of the Lowlands.

Given the context of Allen's life, one might assume that his dec-
laration was limited to the political tempest roiling Vermont at the
time. Further, one might reasonably conclude that Allen's call found
its origin in the Biblical citation of I Kings and that he read it or heard
it preached. While Allen lived in a period with a vastly more religious
timber and one apt to interpret the words more expansively, one can-
not conclude that he meant much more beyond the political implica-
tions pertinent to the turmoil of Vermont then current.

Nevertheless, the declaration and the conflict it represents
continues to reverberate today. It is an ageless battle between the
people of the hills and those of the lowlands. Scotland, Wales and
England, Kashmir and India, Afghanistan and just about everybody
around it, the Caucus and Russia, the peoples of I Kings. Or of the
deserts and wastes in contention with the rich river valleys and coastal
plains. Rome and the invading Teutonic hordes. Or the political rift in
our own society today between blue states and red states, the coasts
and the wide stretch of continent between the two great chains of
the Appalachian Mountains and the Sierras. Parallels exist in the
world of myth; the Aesir and Vanir, the waves of invaders pushing the
indigenous peoples off the good land and into the rugged hills and
mountains.

This conflict has created a far-ranging battlefield. The artifices
of the lowlanders are codified in the term "civilization" and is set in
opposition to the wild, untamed and generally simpler practices of

the "barbarian" or highlander. The garden or the wilderness. The artifices of civilization or the natural world of the savage. Town versus Country. Eventually, the dialogue can be distilled down to Art versus Nature.

In that context, man is pulled back and forth. He is twisted and warped by the conflict. He is pummeled, pounded, and ultimately pulverized by polarizing and seemingly irreconcilable opposites.

Perhaps it is only self-knowledge and the calming self-identity emerging from that knowledge which provides a possible path to reconcile such radically polarized positions, to reach some semblance of harmony, balance, and peace.

The nature of man is not easily discerned. It is a confusing collage of material. Certain elements have little, if any, *nexus* with other elements. Some conflict without hope of reconciliation. Others are hidden underneath newer additions. Some are jarring in color. Some create too much friction. Some are fractured. Some are broken. Some are just plain shattered.

There are certain elements of man's nature, however, which are so beautiful as to take away one's breath. There is harmony, wholeness, and a host of other attributes which only the Divine could produce.

Parsing through this mass of material is a challenge. Application of multiple perspectives helps – and confuses. Proximity produces one interpretation. Distance another. And the multitude of observation points along that spectrum complicates the conclusion. Or conclusions.

There are, perhaps, only three great issues in religion: (1) what is the nature of God; (2) what is the nature of man; and (3) what is the nature of the relationship between the two. These three issues are interdependent, although the nature of God is certainly the foundation upon which the other two are predicated but one never to be plumbed completely.

Ultimately, man's journey here, his or her pilgrimage, is to return to the "Garden," to return to that Paradise Lost, to reach the perfect atonement, that perfect at-one-ment.

Mankind is a dour, crusty, fragile, ragged and quivering collection of pilgrims. Man's nature is complex and confused. The collage is not readily interpreted.

Pilgrimage is characterized by, among other things, the concepts of progress, development, unfoldment, and even creation. Nor did God's creative nature stop at day six. It continues to bloom, to create, to bring fruition. And mankind manifests that creative intent.

For limited mortals, transcendent perception is evasive. The answer to the question as to the nature of man is obscured by the fog. One hopes to catch vague glimpses through the glass darkly, but such sightings are few and fuzzy at best. Further, mortal limitations restrict mankind to a mundane place, a mundane perspective, and a mundane level of understanding.

Much of man's nature becomes visible only in the context of lives experienced, the trials and tribulations, the triumphs and loves. Among the tools of discernment are religion, mythology, and the modern lens of psychology. History and its dynamics become discernable by the themes and motifs which appear. And by their manifestation, they bring structure and order to the wild and chaotic.

Poetry is framed by such context. The words used are derived from particular experiences and individualized more than realized. Dictionaries exist for a purpose; to unify the collective understanding of words - thus confirming that there is an individualization of meaning attributable to each. However, dictionaries also provide light *via* their etymologies as to why certain words resonate so deeply in the human soul. Meanings well from deep pools. Jung's archetypes and their mythic representations are applicable to a wider universe. But poetry's music is universal and of the Divine.

Each steps out his or her life's dance within the Great Dance. The music is of the Divine, and it manifests itself in ways recognizable even if not initially understandable. Thankfully, the manifestations are individualized, and each eventually can find his or her own balance and the rhythm.

Not since the days of hunting and gathering so many eons ago has mankind been so mobile as a society. As a consequence, great benefits have run to society such as diversity, fertile creativity, and economic efficiency. The rewards are manifested in such glorious accomplishments as democracy, mega-cities, and developments in art, literature, science and technology, and a standard of living beyond that ever dreamed.

Glorious. Absolutely glorious.

And yet . . ., roots have been lost. Mankind are now nomads, wanderers through wastes and deserts not necessarily of Nature, although Nature certainly has been raped. Connection with family, friends and the soft familiarity of hearth and home have all been lost. The mountain fastness has been left – and lost.

By definition, roots require a stasis of location. And that "place" becomes "home" in the soul.

All are in exile in one form or another. Place, home, friends, family. Moorings of civility, community, and caring have slipped.

Yet words recall that which has been lost. Words resonate. And poetry amplifies words into a deeper music.

The Taconics are a range of mountains which run along the extreme western border of Vermont down through Massachusetts and finally dissipate in Connecticut. In Vermont, they are part of the Green Mountains. In Massachusetts, they are considered part of the Berkshires. There are various spellings such as *Taghonic* and *Tackonic*.

There are three primary types of trout in the Northeast. There are Brown Trout (*Salmo trutta*), Rainbow Trout (*Oncorhynchus mykiss*), and Brook Trout (*Salvelinus fontinalis*). Only the Brook Trout is native to the territory and is actually a char, although it is related to the trout family. The other two were introduced during the 1800's. The Latin for the Brook Trout, *Salvelinus fontinalis*, is translated *trout of the fountain* which means trout of the springs which create the many small mountain brooks. Please note the role of springs in mythology.

There are so many people to thank; people who gave a kind word, people who contributed in one way or another, directly or indirectly, tangibly or intangibly. There is so much for which I am grateful and so many people to whom I owe so much.

A short list of those to whom I am indebted – in no particular order:

Meghan, Kelsey, Elizabeth, Kristan, M. & P. Linde, V. & M. Matsui, B. E. Donovan, G. Russom, J. Krul, R. Rock, G. "Pequest" Roche, N. Lewis, D. & A. Hemenway, L. M. Peace, D. "Dingle" Davenport, J. DeMarco, D. Rhoads, D. Rondeau, B. LaRoche, K. Harold, P. Lynch, D. Barile, and so many, many others . . ..

This we learned from famous men,
Knowing not we learned it . . ..

Rudyard Kipling

This book is dedicated to the two Lights of my life; Meg and Kels – two angels of God who saved me. I am truly blessed. God's Grace is very great.

BOOK 1
THE TACONICS

AMBER RIVER
(*Uisgabacg*)

With the early morning sun slanting through the trees,
The smooth river becomes a warm amber color,
And I drink in the smell of water reeds,
And the peaty scents of field and forest.

I drink deep of the sun, the river and smells,
I drink deep of the fields and forests and mountains high,
I drink deep of the blue, blue sky,
And am drunk on it all.

Usigabacg is Gaelic for *water of life* and is the word from which is derived the word *whiskey*.

August 1998

BITTER WATERCRESS

The cool waters flow over the sandy-bottomed river
Distilled waters murl and purl
Long banners of green watercress
Wave in the gentle furling currents.
A woven tapestry of water and weed.
Limestone sweetened water.

Thick-flanked trout weave in and out
Munching on sowbugs, pink-bodied crustations,
Silent passengers on the green strands.
And the water toothlessly chews on the watercress,
Gumming its green message.

The hero with rattling teeth
Falls deep, deep, deep down
Into the waters of insanity
Into the chaos of the immersive inversion
And its absolute brilliant, reciprocal principle.
Screams smothered in the murmuring purling.
Mad Sweeney, king turned to bird,
Shaking Gilgamesh, man lost to self.

Watercress, balm to cancerous resentments
Banisher of scurvy in blood and brain.
Bitter taste awakens,
Startles understanding.

February 2011

BLIND TROUTING

The trout rests on the bottom of the run
In the deeper channel carved by water and time.
It flicks a fin,
Languidly waves its tail
Undulating in rhythm to the flow
Hiding in the pulsing current.
Maintaining its position
In hydrodynamic stillness.

The trout is all but invisible
Against the rocky bottom
Algae-greened rocks
Brown in the amber water.
Only a shadow gives the trout away
Revealing the invisible.

A shadow of no substance
Reveals the reality.
We grasp for the finned substance
And seek to capture with iron hook
Of reasoned manufacture
That which defies our vision.

March 2012

COLD WATER

November marches towards winter quarters;
Trees are bare, their autumnal majesty
Now faded and littered on the hard ground.
Bushes and marshes have had their finery stripped,
And puritan grays and browns abound.

The march is halted for one day;
While a gentle sigh warms the land.
A hazy light stops it all mid-step,
Freezing time in its warming embrace;
The air so soft, so sweet, so mild.

Yet while the air holds all apace with airy lies,
The water flows unabated.
Its coldness sharp and unconcerned
By gentle sighs above its ken.
The water cold continues on its way.

Enfolded in the warming arms of a diffused sun,
I smell the air ripe with plant detritus.
And am kissed by fickle breezes fine.
In the river by my feet, the trout
Wedge in deep not fooled by promises fair.

March 2007

THE CUSP

There's a fey light at October's end
A soft gold, a hazy glow,
Warmth lingering from summer
A tease, a dream, a memory
A moment of tranquility
Holding in stasis, a moment's breath
Held in the cusp
Before tumbling into winter's maw.

December 2010

FLUTTERING LEAVES

Under the bright blue sky of October
There is a gentle rain
Of fluttering leaves
Flashing gold, then dark,
Gold, then dark
In their dancing descent.
Others float swaying back and forth,
Back and forth;
Different steps but the same dance
    And the same music.

The forest floor is a fertile book,
A mottled mix of leaves;
Sunlight and shadow.
Each leaf a life,
Each life a leaf
Come to rest at last
In earth's soft embrace.

Sunlight and shadow,
Gold, then dark,
Are the covers of the brittle lives
Littering the forest floor.
Different pages, steps,
But the same dance
    And the same music.

I hold these leafy psalms
In the deep wells
Of memory and soul.
And I dance in the dance
    And sing the same song.

October 2013

HOOKING UP UNDER THE STATION CLOCK

We agree to meet at the station
under the four-faced clock perched
twenty feet up on a fluted pillar
like a dark osprey, watching,
waiting, for the right time to strike.

Under the clock fin a hover
of commuters waiting for
trains, loves, opportunities, ...

But the clock structures, limits,
enmeshes with nets of time,
like Caesar's squared stones, straight
roads on a curved primordial land.
Outside, the train's steel tracks
seek to bind a soft land,
while native paths run along
the watershed's veins and bones,
time measured by flow,
fast here, slow there.

Four-eyed Janus
brooks no rebellion;
the trains keep the schedule
bound by time's tight lines, in four dimensions.
The countless trout-*tuathe* live in
the cold, living current.
Roads crumble under time but
rivers carve their own way.

I leave before the appointed hour
to swim upstream.

Tuathe – Gaelic for *folk, people*. Often used to refer to The Little People (elves, faeries, etc).

May 2007

INDIAN SUMMER

Frost's first waggish kiss
Has come and pricked me,
But the day's resurging warmth
Has dulled the sting.

The sunlight of Indian Summer's final day
Lingers one last golden-ripe moment
Treasuring the stillness of the now,
The last breath of day's absolute essence.

This is summer's farewell embrace;
A slow caress, muted gold,
The failing light of half-tones,
As thought and life fade elsewhere.

October 2009

IRON COWS

The rolling herds of iron cows
Thunder down the asphalt pastures
Seeking wider fields of dreams
But corralled into narrow feeds
Of others' purpose.

Instinct to roam large thwarted,
Dreaming about being horses,
But fated to be bovines.
Bright eyes melt into sad softness.

December 2006

LONG LIGHT

The long light of golden evening
At summer's lingering end.
Time slowing to a hush,
A stillness, ...

The air is warm
Fierce heat just a tanned memory.
Patches of shadows
Stretching into streaks.
Sun-draped lawn
Eroded by evening's shade.
A haunting song of the Green Man
And a day vibrant and abundant.

Rooted hayfield
Stalks heavy with kernels ripe.
A sea of grain
Soon to be shorn and shrived,
Swaying softly with the dance
That will inexorably lead me
Out of the pause
Into the deeper peace.

    . . . Yet,
The light is different
Angled to the south – just a bit
A different hue
A different heft.
Time has slowed

To the season's edge
Lingering in summer dreams
Before tipping into the fall.
A hint of sharp air
And of sleep to come,
The long slow sleep
Of white winter's somnolent snows.

Still, I linger in the now
Savoring the last fruits
Of summer's glory,
At peace in the setting sun
And death's inevitability.

September 2013

MOUNTAIN SPRING

Mountains bleed water,
Rivulets without count
Ooze from the rock.

Cascading necklaces adorn the hillside
Multitudes of sparkling rivulets
Tumble down over rocks,
Twigs, leaves and forest detritus.

Life-giving water,
Blood from the mountains
Washing away winter's white sins.

Sparkling water,
Malleable diamonds of water
And glistening light.
The blood of life
Spilling down the mountainsides;
Catalyst of spring's exuberant dance.

March 2011

NIGHT'S HISTORY

In careful silence, I edge through the door
And out of the house into a cool stillness.
A faint light is etched on the far horizon
While above stars still twinkle brightly
Strewn in abundance beyond measure
Over heaven's celestial gauze.

The air is crisp but moist
And carries traces of I know not what.
The dark trees are silent witnesses
Spilling no secrets, telling no tales.

The invisible air journals the night
Events and participants wrapped in the darkness
Hidden in the nothingness of night.
Yet they were there
And I know them not.

December 2010

SEASONS ARE TURNING

Here and there
A tree has brown leaves,
Dried, stiff, brittle
Too early.

The light in the sky,
Is at a different angle,
Traveling in a shifting arc,
Defused into a softer aura.

Time is refracting,
Autumn slipping forward,
Cooler air whispering,
Seasons are turning.

Seasons are turning.
Trees will don new robes
Of majestic death.
Seasons are turning.

September 2011

SEASONS TURN

Adorned in Indian Summer,
The late afternoon fades
Towards a cold November night.

The low-setting sun
Breathes a soft, warm kiss,
A final blessing for the day
As a pack of chill breezes
Prowl day's perimeter.

Hearing the lingering tattoo,
I tarry on the way
To my sheltering refuge
From winter's ravenous armies
Waiting, for now,
Just across the border.

November 2010

SUN HAS DECLINED

The sun has declined beyond,
But the sky is still light.
A thick lace of silhouetted trees
With a network of intertwined branches.

Memories of rich summer,
A profusion of life
Thick, dense, vibrant
Now disappeared.

Day fades and even the bare trees
With their empty boughs and branches
Merge into the shadows,
And all life slips into the silence
Of cold night.

November 2011

TROUT POOL IN A STAND OF MOUNTAIN PINE

Amber whiskey
Trickling down a rocky course
Tripping over boulders
Sliding through pools
Moments of slow water
Catching its breath
After a rocky tumble.

Tall pines
Golden light filtering through
The green canopy,
Warming the water
With its hallowed fire.

Native brook trout
Tarry in the languid stretch
Drinking the water of life.

March 2011

WHITE CLOUDS ON BLUE SKY

Grey clouds breaking up;
Cracking, fracturing, crumbling,
Tumbling down, tearing apart,
Shattered into shards.
Low grey clouds trampled by
The racing white mares above.

Beyond the blaring mares
Bright blue sky,
A spring blue, a royal blue,
A blue of spring and first flowers,
A blue of spring and fertility;
The regal mating of king and land,
The white horse on a royal blue field.
The white horse on a royal blue bed.

March 2011

WINTER DAWN

The dawn is still,
A bold pink is smeared across the east
And tinged with red to strengthen;
Then stiffened with an edge of ancient bronze.

Silence echoes amongst the bare trees.
The cold digs deep into bones
And clings to the tucks and folds
Of the land's snow-covered wrinkles.

March 2010

A WINTER NIGHT'S TAIL

There are several hours still
Until dawn's heralded arrival.
Darkness reigns supreme.
Glittering stars glorify
Night's infinite black.
The cold air grips all in thrall;
Hard despite being of no substance.

With no lights on,
I sit by the window
Looking out onto the night
Clutching my coffee mug close
Letting the heat well up
Onto my face.
The aroma percolates
Into my mind
Still stumbling after sleep's embrace.

Night is the negative space,
That which is the void
   tween the substance we see.
    that which has no form,
    upies no space in its own right,
     s only the absence of something else.

There is much empty space
In the world, in body, in mind,
In which I exist or don't.
Nameless, formless, unknown
In this night, at this hour.

December 2013

WINTER'S FIRST STORM

Winter's first storm slams into the hill
Rampaging through the trees
Flinging them back and forth
Tearing off the last lingering leaves
With a rabid ravenousness.

The cold wind charges the house
Hurtling itself upon the fragile structure
Shaking its very beams
Gnawing on every loose shutter
With an insatiable hunger.

Angry sleet hammers the tin roof
Building redoubts of ice
Seeking its way inside
To pillage and plunder
In savage inhuman fury.

December 2010

YELLOW FORSYTHIA

The yellow forsythia
Have burst into fountains
Of shocking brightness
After never-ending greyness.

I am shaken
Out of my daze
By such raw vitality.
Spring blaring
Life trumpeting
In wild abandon.

Depression dissipates
And I arise
To the new day.

April 2013

BOOK 2
THE SON OF MAN

A BAPTISM OF DROWNING

Fate, or perhaps fear,
Cast me adrift one dark night
Into a vaster sea beyond my ken
Without dimensions or buoys.
Raw water thrashes my fragile bark.
My craft is of naught
To ride the tempest, or tame it.
But I cannot leave the fragile vessel
And walk across the sharp-peaked waves
Through the hurtling storm,
The wind-whipped walls of wet terror,
Formlessness poised to crush form into pulp.
Fear grinds dreams into nightmares
As Light's child struggles to stay afloat
Only to disappear into the water's fierce grip.

The mathematician wrestles
With the error solved at Peniel:
Two plus two equals four.
Peace, be still, he commands.
Principle expressed solves the equation.
Law draws up the quivering wreck.
The waters subside, winds abate,
And the drowning soul, now baptized,
Dances o'er the laughing white-caps
Sparkling in the Light.

September 2011

THE BURNING BUSH

I did my hunting at dawn's first light,
High up the hills along fields' edge.
I sought to flush the birds to flight,
And shoot them with my Savage.

The Son of man strode through the meadows,
A mighty swagger swinging with a shotgun.
I walked right through the shadows;
Fields and forests, clothes and mind, all in dun.

In a silent roar sprung forth the light,
As the Sun jumped o'er the mountain.
Shadows were vanquished from all sight.
The woodchuck scampered from his den.

At fields' edge in Fall's regal robes,
A bush burned up before my eyes,
Yet consumed not were any leaves.
I looked up and searched the skies.

On holy ground I stood entranced,
The voice of God before me.
The earth stopped still and balanced,
My life to spare could I only plea.

October 1992

THE DANCE OF TIME

Time constrained and bound me in,
With airy bonds of windy disbelief,
I writhed within my dark prison,
Hemmed into thoughts too brief.

Time does dance a swirling step,
Of thoughtless manner, speed and stage.
Her robes flowed past as I watching wept,
Dancing an ageless cage of age.

Time does dance within my mind,
An enchanting pattern of size and shape,
All wov'n at speeds to make me blind,
And struggle madly in 'tangling tape.

Time knows no manner, speed or stage.
They never did go dance with her.
For she never lived beside my rage,
All four a whispered murmur.

No date.

DARK HOUNDS

The dark hounds hurtle down upon me,
Fearsome foaming fanged fiends.
Rolling red tongues,
Hard muscled hounds hunting down their mark.

I madly run and scramble,
In fear-lust drenched,
Heart straining to escape,
In futile steps and leaps.

My fears race after me,
In fevered rabid madness.
I seek to flee them,
In a frantic mindless sprint.

But they will dog my trails,
Lunging at my heels,
'Til the cool winds come to calm,
And I turn upon the tail.

December 1991

THE CRY

The cry rocketed off the wall,
Piercing my heart with her pain.
The tears cascaded down,
Searing salt from a sinless innocent.

I hover to give succor,
In futile attempts to calm and heal,
But no mortal aid can restore,
Pure innocence lost.

Forgive me, my sweet babe,
I prayed to be allowed,
Your pain to shoulder,
But your life and its all,
    Is for you alone.

January 1992

BITTERSWEET

I got up early to see you off
On your first day of school,
When you left for college,
On the first day of your summer job.

I made the coffee strong,
Thick and pungent.
It bit my tongue,
Scalded my throat.

The coffee distracts me
From self-centered grief;
Not for my own diminishing years
But my grief for your absence,
And as I rejoice
For your lengthening days of glory.

March 2011

DAY'S LABORS

The day's labors over,
I lie on the hard bed
Of my regrets
Seeking solace and relief
In sleep's forgetfulness.

The world spins
Ever faster, ever tighter, and
The tides of starry seas pound
The fragile soul's rocky coast.

I fall into pools of failure,
Dark currents of despair,
A mortal man
Contesting the cosmic chaos.
How droll.

Finally, I fall asleep
To mocking laughter
And my own folly.

July 2013

DEAD TREE

The sky trumpeted a bright blue
A strong sun showered brightness.
Yet the sky was not blue enough
And the sun was not bright enough,
And darkness ruled.

With bare feet
The child padded along an asphalt road
Which led into the deep forest
Blue sky and bright sun
Hidden by the thick canopy.
Dark mysteries, holy ground,
Barefoot in the cathedral before God.

The child disappeared into the sacred forest
Heart ripped apart by sadness
And loneliness and fear and pain
Without end.

The child walked under the holy trees
That arched overhead like a cathedral,
A holy sanctuary on the path.
The child could take no more,
The pain and suffering a cold fire.
The child kissed a tree,
A long lingering shattering moment
Dangled on the end of a rope.
Embraced the tree in an explosion of hurtling steel
Collapsed on its roots by poison foul;
The child kissed the tree.

And life by life, soul by soul,
The universe withers.
The family of man is diminished.
Each destroyed leaf
A void not to be refilled.
And I howl for the lost soul,
For that beautiful child
Now gone.

September 2011

DOWN, DOWN

Down, down the mountainside
Tumbles the Son of Man.
Rain slicks the jagged scree,
Torrents grab at ankles,
And pull feet out from under.

Body is bashed,
Against laughing boulders.
Flesh is pounded,
Bones are broken,
As down the mountain he falls.

Ever growing waters,
Engorged by the storm's spawn,
Crash into each other,
Smashing and slashing,
And sweep the Son of Man on.

Spewed out into the mighty seas,
The undertow finishes the destruction,
And the body churns round and around,
And pulp dissolves into pap,
And pap into nothingness.

And who says
The King is dead,
Long live the King!
But him who sought the King to kill.

July 2010

FISHER KING

He fishes in a broken river;
Tumbled by rocks;
Malleable water of iron will
Leaves leg broken.

The kingdom is broken
And Everyman suffers
From the wounds;
Lines unmendable in crashing currents.

Kingdom of dirt,
Desert kingdom,
Harsh land of unforgiving stone;
Water banked rigidly.

Angling t'wixt water, rock and light.
He limps as he wades
In the currents too deep.

He waves his greenwood scepter
From which extends the iron hook;
Reason's manufactured vanity
Employed to predatory purpose.

Thirst unfulfilled.
The void so obvious
And so unfathomable.
Root knowledge sought
To recover the Lost.

Broken within,
He seeks to catch the piscator king;
To heal the kingdom
And himself.

March 2012

GOD'S CHILD

I wake during night's darkest embrace,
Sleepless, I wander onto the back porch,
Wrapped in a blanket against the chill,
A formless shape, in darkness I sit.

I look up into the star-strewn void,
That runs beyond my ability to understand,
Other than my own incalculable insignificance,
As my soul is swallowed up in the infinitude.

Pilloried by this irrelevance,
My soul shrinks,
And I am humbled into dirt.

. . .

Slowly, forces greater than myself
Bring light to the east.
Night wanes, dawn waxes.
The last stars slip from sight.

Heaven's dome is cloaked in royal blue,
My sun ascends.
My shapeless form previously wrapped in blackness,
Emerges to discernment.

August 2009

THE GREEN MAN RETURNS – 1

On the high bare ridge-line,
Near the top of the heavy-shouldered mountain
Where worn bones of mountain stone
Burst from the thin mantle of dirt,
There passed an odd figure;
Perhaps a man.

He stumbled along the sharp crest,
Or perhaps it was a dance he stepped
T'wixt rock and dour sky.
He passed from sight in just a moment
And all was as it was before.

Yet wasn't.

December 2010

THE GROCER

It is a small shop
Squeezed between
Two large meccas
Of clothes and liquor.

The grocer brandishes his broom
Belligerently sweeping the sidewalk
Futilely banishing the mess before his stalls.
He's a rotund little fellow
Not unlike the small spuds.

I wonder at the mess,
The unending chaos,
Which tumbles me and this world.
Puny human strength
Of no consequence
In the cosmic maelstrom;
Tempests and turmoil; principle fractured.

I look at the ordered ranks of apples
Subtle variations of reds, pinks, yellows,
Colors singing so beautifully.
Full-bodied, ripe fruit
The righteous fruitage of a lone seed
Planted so many years ago.
Vitality resplendent bent in a tiny, dark kernel
That has yielded the impossible harvest before my eyes
By forces and powers beyond my ken.

Trucked in from unknown distant places,
The apples are stacked neatly,
A structured manifestation
In a crazed world.

The grocer whistles
As he sorts through a box of pears.

December 2013

THE HALF-SPACE

The great ocean, steel blue,
Chanting in sonorous curl,
Tickles the bleached sand,
Stone worn down by wind and wave.

T'wixt righteous rock and iron sea,
Small children gamble,
In the half-space,
At ease in the ambiguity.

Tousled hair is streaked
By salt and sun.
Skin is browned and glowing,
With white strips peaking,
From under slipping clothes,
Stretched by movement free.

The salt-tinged breeze,
With the white-lipped wave,
Sings with the children's clear laughter,
And I listen and joy,
And mourn what I no longer am.

August 2009

LETTING GO

Letting go,
Tearing the heart asunder.
Why, I cannot ken.
I throw myself onto the bed of nails,
Spear-points plunging straight through,
Laced with burning salt
And acid venom.

I can't open my hand,
Release my grip.
My hand has to be severed
Before I can let go.

And the pain
The pain . . .
Of such an intense vibration,
As pure as a clear bell's note,
That completely shatters me
Into shards of atoms.

And I know not why . . ..

March 2012

LIFE PRESERVER

Life preserver, white plastic
Ever-buoyant, ever-ready,
Hangs on the wall.
A mess of rope
Is festooned in a jumble
On the rim, on the hook, on the ground.

Within the circle of the preserver,
A spider has spun a silky web
In ordered lines
Of geometric wisdom.
The creature's wisdom
Makes a mockery of mine.

A life was lost this summer
A young girl's
Snarled in webs of chemicals
Too strong to break
Too chaotic for a young mind
To comprehend, to understand.

There was no life preserver,
No response to cries for help
In waters too deep.
It just hung on the wall
Festooned with a jumble of rope;
An unclear mind, a chaotic mind.

September 2011

LINEAR CAIRN

The old linear cairn
Silently cuts through the dense woods
Reclaiming their kingdom
From long-dead famous men.

The wall is half-buried
In the snow
Brought by the ancient North Wind
Obliterating half the wall from view
In blank white drifts.

Wasted fields,
Fruitless labor,
Decapitated ambition,
Forgotten life.

January 2011

THE MOMENT

In the early morning,
The air is still
Held in freshness,
Cool and slightly damp.

The world is poised
In a perfect balance
Of the moment.
The rotating axis has stopped.
Time stands still
In the moment.
Only the birds sing,
Pure notes transcending
The moment.

I breathe in the air.
I breathe in the notes.
I merge into the moment.

April 2012

MOONLIGHT ON MARINES

The moonlight seeps through the trees,
Spilling on the line of men.
A company strong threading their way,
Through the hills and vales.

Against the green blackness of the night,
The pale luminescence brings an eerie contrast.
Troops of trees and platoons of marines,
Still trees, marching men.

Humping heavy packs,
Weighed down with gear,
Rifles cradled in arms,
Minds vigilant in the night movement.

The trees watch the passing men,
Envying their freedom of limb,
Yet not the weight on the supple frames,
Their own a leafy lightness.

The moon shines down
And washes o'er the men
Grim in their purpose,
Solid in their hearts.

The moon shines down,
Bathing the trees.
Trees and men, all silent,
Purpose driven.

No date.

MORNING COFFEE

It's dark as I turn on the coffee pot.
The heater hums, the water gurgles,
Air hiccups and hisses.
I hover feeding on the aroma.

I float in the silence of the pre-dawn,
The cusp of half-light,
Shadowed dreams.
The light washes the sleeping world,
Soft caresses to waken.

I lean against the hard-edged counter.
The ethereal fades
Into the mundane of iron appliances.

The coffee fumes float up,
Heated dancers in the chill night air.
My hands grasp the warm mug.
I huddle over the nourishing aroma.

Wraith-like, I feed off the aroma
Finding nourishment.
Flesh and blood emerge from the ether.
No more dancing among the stars,
Grounded in the day.

September 2011

THE OLD MARINE

The old man hobbles down the aisle,
Ankle throbbing
From the morning's spill;
Ligaments clawing at muscles
Twisting all the way up the leg
To where part was carved out
By a bullet.
Memory still bloody,
Pain still present.

February 2012

ROLL WIND

Roll wind, roll wind roll.
Slap me with your chill barbs.
Flay skin from flesh
And flesh from bone.
Tear my mind from its skull.

Roll wind roll.
Smash the waves into the rock.
Crumble the continent
Grain by grain.
Race against erupting molten furies.

Roll wind roll.
Flatten fields of hay;
Stalks are stiff.
Topple towering trees;
Roots are not deep,
Wood is brittle.
Topple crowns off swelling heads.

April 2010

ROTTED TREE

Leaves so green,
A lacy filigree
Fluttering bravely
Masking lies.

A howling devil
Snarling and laughing in a fell voice
Toppled it, snapped the massive trunk,
Wind's iron jaws crunched
Ripping open the hollow guts.

Mighty tree,
Once so proud and tall
Now so broken and low;
Ashamed of its false colors.

The nut fell away
As the tree toppled,
Rolled away from the sin.
Its turn to better its sire.

August 2010

SLAVE

The young man sits outside
Puffing away on a butt
During his mandated break.

His body is old before its time
Despite the regular, hard exercise after hours.
His mind is atrophied.
His spirit ground down.

A slave of the machine,
He smokes in the sunshine
Drugged into compliance,
Wasting away his life and body
Despite the singing sunshine.

He lights a second cigarette
Breathing the smoke
Deep into his lungs
Before returning
To his cage of a cubicle.

March 2012

STRETCHING FOR THE DAWN

Night's fevered dreams
Mercilessly drive me
Into anguish and anxiety,
Torturing my slumbering soul.

Wolves howl in the darkness
Tracking me down
Getting closer and closer.

I wake in a sweat,
Heart pounding from the hunt.
Dark dreams evaporate in the light;
Wolves skewered by sunbolts.
Fingers stretch for the dawn;
Sunlight, mercy, and salvation.

January 2013

TAG SALE

An erratic dribble of foragers flow through
Half-heartedly picking over the displayed detritus
Of the widow's life.
Bits and pieces; a broken silver mirror from a make-up table,
Baby toys for children long gone,
Glass dessert dishes, one chipped.
A big pot for large family meals no longer used.
Her life laid out to be fingered, evaluated, and judged
By those oblivious to the life behind each object.

As the buyers funnel out each with a salvaged piece,
A little bit of her heart ebbs out with them,
A tiny part of her life leaving.

They tell her she is freeing herself
Divesting herself of weighty matter
Of items no longer of consequence.
But her heart wails otherwise,
And a chill envelops her.

January 2012

TREE TALK

The trees talk to me,
And tell me much
If I have but the wit to listen.

They tell me from where the wind is blowing,
They point where is north,
They warn me of August's thunderstorms,
They sing me the changes of the seasons.

Trees have voices;
Some soft and rustling,
Some rough and barky.
They tell me much,
These voices of the trees.

I place my ear aside a trunk;
Woody hide, jagged skin.
I hear the voice inside the tree,
Singing, laughing to me.

I am a *wodhu* of the woods,
My kingdom a leafy one,
Like Sweeney or Grendel.
I live no more with men,
And think my green world
Far sweeter and they insane.

July 2010

TRUCKLE

I watch her sitting, bound to her desk,
Head down, back bent,
Mesmerized in the numbing task at hand,
Churning paper, filing reports,
On paper churned and reports filed.

I watch an ant laboring,
Body rigid,
Subsumed in the allocated task,
Lugging a corpse back to the nest,
Mindless automaton bringing back food.

September 2009

WORN OUT

She labors without rest
Scrubbing to clean
The impossibly dirty,
Struggling to take away
The endless pain of others
Into her own wounded heart.

Tears have long since dried up,
The wells exhausted,
Physically, emotionally.

The light flickers
A shadow now
Which once shone so clearly.
So bright a note
Now muffled darkness.

March 2012

BOOK 3
PILGRIMAGE

BRIDGE

We wander in a wan land,
A waste of dark desolation,
Struggling through war's slurry
Of decomposing corpses and dread dreams,
Thick and grasping.

A small hole poked through
The storm-howling clouds above.
A slender shaft of shining light,
A merciful spear of pointed love,
Kissed my hammered brow.

A touch of grace beyond my hope,
A gift to me beyond my ken,
A gift not to be wasted,
Given for a purpose.

Little difference between
Me and the mud;
So little difference between
Me and the corpses already there.

Graced by the light
I lie down in the muck
My body a bridge
For others to escape.

November 2013

DAY FOLLOWS NIGHT

Darkness still rules
When I rise for the day
Faithing that day will in truth appear.

Day follows night
And night follows day
In a great wheeled voyage
Beyond my ken.

But I run with it
Confident, optimistic,
As I sip the scalding coffee
And await Dawn's appearance;
Knowing that time
Is distance measured
On the pilgrim path.

April 2013

THE FINGERPRINT OF GOD

T'was a bright sunny morn in June,
Or perhaps July, I really don't recall,
When I set out to build,
An equation just for fun.

I built myself an algorithm,
Filled with 2's and 3's and 7's,
And lots of x's and lots of y's,
To n degrees refined.

It was a light little thing
Rather short and temporary,
Meant for a light-hearted morning's amusement,
To pass the time away.

I dallied in the rich summer meadows,
And idly took its derivative,
Finding a line most pleasing,
To my casual eye.

I thought about the algorithm,
About that equation's infinite line,
And then about the infinite derivative,
And the second derivative, in turn.

Derivatives piled upon derivatives,
An infinite plethora of infinite lines,
And then for laughs, I thought about,
The underivative, too.

What a tangle of lines,
I thought to myself,
As I laid aside the mess.
Too much for me to bother about,
On a day as merry as this.

Back I went for simplicity's sake,
To the very first algorithm,
And carefully traced its linear passage,
Through the pages of my mind.

An infinite line, I thought to myself,
Must pass some pretty fun places.
Why, perhaps there's a circle,
Tangent right here and one right there.

Circles and circles all over the place,
All with their mysterious pi,
A value of substance yet never resolved;
A ridiculous treasure it seems.

Then circles upon circles,
Roared out "What ho!"
And they filled up my mind.
Tangent at each tiny spot,
On the whole long line, and
Then on each derivative, and
Then on each derivative piled on each derivative, and
Underivatives, too,
Lay circle upon circle.

Chaos it seemed,
With lines and circles all amuck,
And endless confusion,
Extending beyond my sight.

And the mass of the lines and circles,
Grew heavy and passed from
My mind as the lines
Cut across time.
New circles came forth, then
Sank away in turn,
And new dimensions were seen,
As the mass of the circles,
Warped thought all around.

Madness crept in and smiled at me slyly,
As I sought to keep a grasp,
On the slippery mess.
"Let go. Just let go. Slide down to the whole."
All I could see were lines and circles,
Falling into a very small hole,
Black as the void.

September 1994

FOLLOW THE TRAIL

I follow the trail up
Running alongside the cascading brook
Hopping back and forth
From bank to bank
Over tumbling water
And cracked stones
From the crumbling mountain
Which slash the water
Into rivulets and fractions of sparkling light.

    The clock chimes the hour.
    Time has marked off
    Its own self-delineating existence;
    Madness of self now defined.

I follow the trail up
Brook and path crossing each other
Merging the journey.
Land and water
Both tripped up
By cracked stones
From the crumbling mountain
Which mix the worlds of land and water
Into a jumbled, tumbled pathway
Down the mountainside,
A braided course.
Strands of existence woven together
Into a fabric of experience.

The old man lifts the wine
Bottle straight to lips.
A rill dribbles
Down his chin onto his ragged clothes.

I follow the trail up
Fighting falling rock and water,
Climbing against the currents
Of water, gravity and obstructing mountain
That would keep me wallowing
In the lowlands
Where the waters are still
And the land washed flat
With broken mountain ground fine.

The kitchen is warm
With the smells of cooking;
While woodchucks howl
From the surrounding forest.

I follow the trail up.
Mountain bone bare
In its elemental purity,
Unsoftened by time,
Scoured by the elements.

The babe gurgles and coos,
Soft skin and silky hair,
While the white-maned croon
Coos into her ear.

I follow the trail up,
Am likewise purged by the path.
Lowland dross scraped off
By hard, sharp stone
And water's razor edge.

    Layers of skin
    Peeled off.
    Excruciating pain.
    Death would be a release.

I follow the trail up,
Breaking out from under
Forest green
Into sky blue.
Am slapped by the hostile wind
Angry at the trespass
Into its kingdom.
Now sullied by my mortal vestments.

    The banshee wails
    At the pain from the lies.

I follow the trail up,
Despite the chill warning,
Into the bright sky.
Drawn inexorably to the royal throne
Willing to hazard the razor's edge
For the eternal kingdom.

The young woman
Stands to the side
Wringing her hands
While she cries
"The king is dead.
Long live the King!"

January 2012

NIGHT'S EDGE

Golden hay bordered by dun trees,
    Fills my eyes with a dusky haze.
Evening's tattoo cascades through my mind,
    As I fall off night's edge.

Yet brambles prick and rend religion's robes,
    While milk pails slosh the frothy feast.
Rivers ramble in midsummer madness,
    As I fall off night's edge.

The meads smell so sweet;
    A heady ale of ambition's spilled blood.
Roads run by the river silly,
    As I fall off night's edge.

I hear the dirge of dismounting iron men.
    Woodchucks howl in their dens.
The trout leap high for pens to touch the sky,
    As I fall off night's edge.

November 1991

OLD GODS WALK THE EARTH

The past is never dead. It's not even past.
William Faulkner

Old gods walk the earth in new guises
    Just look closely.
Old battles are refought on fields
    Of fresh green.
A swath is mown
    Through the heavy-headed stalks.
Crows flap heavily across my path
    Gorged from their meaty feast.

April 2010

OWEN'S LADDER

The little boy squatted
On the freshly-furrowed field.
He picked up a clump of moist earth;
Large clump, small hands.

Chick-a-dee, he warbled,
The only bird song he knew,
And gazed at the royal blue sky
Shining above him.

Idly, he rubbed the dirt
On his skinny bare leg;
New dirt covering the old.
Feral eyes a sandy shade
Seeing the world before him
By being one with it.
No need for a ladder
To heaven's door.

April 2012

THE PILGRIM ROAD TO EDEN

It's an old dream
Going far, far back
On the dusty track that grudgingly stumbles
Over the rolling steppes of wind-whipped grasses,
Across giant, sharp-edged mountains
That with time's grinding fist
Wear down into seas of jagged scree,
And endless deserts of ruthless grit;
All howling wildernesses of terrifying silence.

The iron shoe on the worn staff was
Long since knocked off on a nameless rock,
Cracked skin and croaking voice,
Twisted sinew and blistered sole,
And legend's tattered robe
Barely covers the gaunt limbs
And provides the bones no warmth against
The aching cold of a star-filled night
And the harsh laughter of an absolute cosmos
Peering down from beyond sight.

Walled Vanity squats on a defensible knoll
Overlooking the blood-soaked path
That rabid armies, thin-lipped traders and mad wanderers take.
Smug temples ring hollow bells of cracked brass
To placate red-eyed gods.
Houses wrap around courtyards
Of multi-colored tiles and bubbling fountains.
Vines twist up through trellises,

Sweet-smelling flowers with opulent scents,
Oasis of beckoning comfort,
Subtle temptations to lure the unwary and weary.

The miles are as endless as the mountains
Are without count; heart-breaking climbs
With lung-bursting heights. How can frail flesh refrain,
Weak against temptation's simpering caresses,
Clashing cymbals and refined savories?
Subtle temptations to lure the unwary and weary.

But the waste places call
And unfettered feet stagger on
Climbing toward the hidden pass
That leads . . . we know not where
But can only dream.

April 2008

PRAYERFUL TREE

In the midst of an old field
Long combed and brushed,
Fined and winnowed,
Its stones teased out,
There stood a solitary tree.

Generation after generation
The hay springs forth;
Each stalk topped with a banner of corn,
A memory of mustard seed.

The hay rises but only so high
Its reach for the heavens thwarted,
And the season passes.
The lone tree watches and prays.

Straight stood the Shepherd
Stalwart, free, wood-strong,
Soaring up to the sky.
Limbs stretched up
Reaching, reaching.

No bent boughs,
No twisted trunk,
No limbs gravity-fettered,
Slumped in doleful worship.

But alive in Grace
Joying in life
And bursting with kernel knowledge.
It seeks its Source
With eagerness, with joy, in tree-song
Every leaf a psalm, a song.
Hosanna, Hosanna, Hosanna.

And I now see
How trees pray
And why.

October 2013

UNCERTAIN

Clouds cover the sky and
Darkness retreats stubbornly
Grudgingly conceding only a grey muted dawn.
The air is moist;
Rain is in the offing.
The world is tenuous and muzzy
In the quarter-light.

The path before me
Is dark and unclear.
I test the ground with each step;
Reality is cloaked in hazy ambiguity,
Perception confused
By cloud, mist and shadow.

April 2013

INDEX OF TITLES

INDEX OF FIRST LINES

Made in the USA
Middletown, DE
27 August 2017